Perform a Beautiful
Wedding Ceremony
in Minutes

REV SHERRY HARRISON

Copyright © 2021

REV SHERRY HARRISON

PERFORM A BEAUTIFUL WEDDING CEREMONY IN MINUTES

All rights reserved.

No part of this publication may be reproduced, distributed, or transmitted in any form or by any means, including photocopying, recording, or other electronic or mechanical methods, without the prior written permission of the author, except in the case of brief quotations embodied in critical reviews and certain other non-commercial uses permitted by copyright law.

REV SHERRY HARRISON

Printed in the United States of America
First Printing 2021
Second Edition 2022
Third Edition 2023

ISBN: 979-8715341129

INTRODUCTION

You are ready to perform your first of many weddings with just this one book! I am so excited for you!

My name is Rev Sherry Harrison. I was married in a small chapel in Yuma, Arizona, years ago – 1976, as a matter of fact. I was so in love with the tiny space, it stuck with me. After my children graduated, I just kept building my own chapel in my head. Eventually, I got a job with a gentleman who owned an old church. He officiated at this church and held receptions in the basement using his catering business. I learned a lot. After one year, he sold his church. It was time for me to jump into my dream and open my own little wedding chapel.

I was able to touch the lives of over 800 couples and am so proud of how happy I made them. My concept was always to make a small wedding still feel like they had their dream wedding, for an affordable price. It wasn't about getting rich. It was about giving something beautiful for them to look back on, as I had with my own little wedding, in a little wedding chapel.

My research on wedding scripts led me to write my own more modern and beautiful one. It started out with the basic, non-denominational one pager. Every time a couple asked for something, I researched and added it as an option. So, this book is the culmination of all those options in ceremonial order. By using the instructions and quick checklist in this book with the wedding couple you will have a beautiful, memorable, ready-made wedding for them in minutes!

The author, Rev Sherry Harrison, is not responsible or liable for the legality of weddings you perform.

A special thank you to my son, Andy, and my daughter, Misty.
Without them, this book would not be possible.

How to Use the Checklist to Create a Custom Wedding Ceremony

IMPORTANT! Check with the ceremony location's county court clerk's office for their laws on officiating a wedding.

Make sure you know the state/county laws and requirements:

1. for an officiant to perform a wedding at the couple's ceremony location. (For example, the couple may want to get married in a neighboring state.)
2. for whether it is necessary to obtain certification/s to be ordained. (For example, a state may not require an ordained minister to perform the ceremony.)
3. of the marriage license process (who needs to sign it, when/where to sign on the license, and if witnesses are required) and the time frame for returning the marriage license itself.

****Helpful Hint: Make copies of the <u>blank</u> checklist to use for multiple weddings.***

This ceremony book is configured to be used with male-female couples, LGBTQ+ and non-binary couples.

- A basic non-denominational civil ceremony would use the **black** lettered [non-optional] pages. This basic ceremony takes about 4 minutes.
- Any of the green *optional* pages can be added to a basic ceremony.
- The green *optional* pages with a purple cross (✝) reference God or Prayers for those who want a more religious ceremony.

Go down the checklist with the wedding couple to create their personalized ceremony:

- The first question to ask the couple is if they want the word "God" or prayers in their ceremony. If not, they won't be interested in the optional pages with the purple cross (✝) on pages 6, 7, 17, and 23, nor the word "Holy" on page 4.
- As pages are selected by the couple, blank spaces will need to be filled in with names; [Groom/Person] and [Bride/Person] indicate where their names should be said. Though not necessary, traditionally the groom would be first to say their vows, exchange rings, etc. It is also important to ask the couple what pronouns/words they would like to use. These are in [green brackets] on the following pages: 2, 10, 11, 14, 15, 26, 27.
- On page 26, the officiant will choose to say either "State" or "County" based on where they are approved to perform weddings. There is also a blank space to write the name of the aforementioned state or county [State/County Name].
- You can use sticky notes with their exact choices on every page, so you read it correctly as you go through the ceremony on their wedding day. If this book will only be used for one wedding to become the couple's keepsake, they may want the blank spaces permanently written in the book.
- Some pages have red (pause/actions) indicating where you need to wait for the couple to do something or repeat after you, before you continue on.
- You can always add in additional pages of prayers, songs, acknowledgements, etc. to make the wedding couple's ceremony customized perfectly.

***Helpful Hint**: Use sticky tabs to mark which pages the couple chose. This way you can easily bypass the un-chosen pages while reading their ceremony.*

***Helpful Hint**: Have the Unity Sand/Candle table set up nearby prior to the ceremony beginning. Also, make sure they have a lighter or matches at the table to light the outside candles when it is time.*

CHECKLIST

[✝ denotes referencing God or Prayers]

Page #:

- ☐ 1. The Ceremony is Beginning
- ☐ Optional 2. Giving Bride/Person Away
- ☐ 3. Please Be Seated
- ☐ 4. Officiant's Welcome [✝Holy]
- ☐ 5. Officiant's Opening Words
- ☐ Optional✝ 6.-7. Officiant's Opening Prayer
- ☐ 8. Ask Groom/Person; Do You Take
- ☐ 9. Ask Bride/Person; Do You Take
- ☐ Optional 10. Remembering Those Unable to Attend
- ☐ Optional 11. Honoring Those Who Have Passed
- ☐ 12. Officiant's Intro to Vows
- ☐ Optional 13. Hand in Hand Poem
- ☐ 14. Groom/Person Vows
- ☐ 15. Bride/Person Vows
- ☐ Optional 16. Officiant's Intro to Rings
- ☐ Optional✝ 17. Officiant's Blessing of Rings
- ☐ Optional 18. Groom/Person Gives Ring
- ☐ Optional 19. Bride/Person Gives Ring
- ☐ Optional 20. Sand Unity <u>OR</u> 21. Unity Candle
- ☐ Optional 22. Recognition of Children
- ☐ Optional✝ 23. Officiant's Closing Prayer
- ☐ 24.-25. Officiant's Closing Words
- ☐ 26. Pronouncement of Marriage
- ☐ Optional 27. Presentation

(When the ceremony is ready to begin, walk to the altar, open your book
and smile at your audience. They should quiet down,
but if not, say)

Can we please have quiet; the ceremony is beginning

The Ceremony is Beginning

(the Bride/Person may or may not walk down the aisle)

(once the wedding couple is at the altar, ask)

Who Gives This [Woman/Man/Person]
to be Married to This [Man/Woman/Person]?

(pause for response)

Giving Bride/Person Away

(when the wedding couple is at the altar,
if the audience is standing say)

Please Be Seated

We Have Come Together Today

to Witness the Joining Together of

_____ [Groom/Person Name]

and

_____ [Bride/Person Name]

in [✝ Holy] Matrimony

Officiant's Welcome

This Wedding Ceremony

is the Recognition of a Commitment

That You Have Already Made

in Your Hearts.

Marriage is Built

on Events of Daily Life,

and Grows Strong;

Not Without Challenge

and Adversity,

But With Compromise, Patience,

and Love.

Officiant's Opening Words

✝

God Has Abundantly Blessed
and Enriched Your Lives
in Finding Each Other.
As He Guided Us to This Beautiful Event,
We Give Thanks for His Tender Care
and Eternal Love.

Let Us Pray…

Officiant's Opening Prayer, part 1

✝

Dear Lord,

We Ask That You Bless This Couple With

A True and Understanding Love for Each Other;

That They Be Filled With Faith and Trust.

We Ask That You Grant Them the Grace

to Live With Each Other in Peace and Harmony.

We Ask That You Help Them Exhibit

Patience, Kindness, Cheerfulness,

and the Spirit of Placing the Well-Being

of the Other, Ahead of Self.

We Ask That You Bless This Love

That Brought This Marriage to Be.

Amen

Officiant's Opening Prayer, part 2

_____ [Groom/Person Name]

Do You Take

_____ [Bride/Person Name]

to Be Your Lawfully Wedded;

to Give Your Hand, Your Heart,

and Your Love

Throughout Your Life's Journey

Together?

(pause for response)

Ask Groom/Person, Do You Take

_____ [Bride/Person Name]

Do You Take

_____ [Groom/Person Name]

to Be Your Lawfully Wedded;

to Give Your Hand, Your Heart,

and Your Love

Throughout Your Life's Journey

Together?

(pause for response)

Ask Bride/Person, Do You Take

We Take This Moment to Remember

_____ [Name/s].

[He/She/They] [was/were]

Unable to Attend Today.

We Send Our Heartfelt Thanks for

[His/Her/Their]

Love and Support.

Remembering Those Unable to Attend

We Send Out a Special Tribute to

_____ [Name/s]:

We are Eternally Grateful for

[His/Her/Their]

Loyalty, Friendship, and Love

While on This Earth.

By Remembering the Best of Times,

Recalling [His/Her/Their] Finest Qualities,

Guiding Principles, and Values,

May You Take Away with You

the Noblest Parts

and be Enriched Because of it.

Please Face Each Other,

Join Hands,

and Look Into Each Others' Eyes.

It is Said….

As I Have Given You My Hand to Hold,

So I Give You My Life to Keep.

Officiant's Intro to Vows

We Stand Together, Your Hand in Mine.

Time Matters Not, All is Fine.

The Simple Touch of Skin to Skin,

Stirs a Warmth That Reigns Within.

Hand in Hand, All Barriers Dissolve,

As One We Merge, All Cares Resolve.

From Your Hand to Mine, an Energy Flows,

Filling Our Minds, Hearts, and Souls.

Touching So Close, the World Fades Away.

Reality Dims in Love's Strong Sway.

Words Are Not Needed, None Are Said.

By Just a Touch, Our Souls Are Wed.

Hand in Hand Poem

_____ [Groom/Person Name];

Repeat After Me:

I_____ [Groom/Person Name] (pause)

Choose You _____ [Bride/Person Name] (pause)

to Be My Wedded [Wife/Husband/Spouse]; (pause)

to Share My Life in All Things. (pause)

I Will Love You and Cherish You (pause)

With Honor and Respect; (pause)

for Better and for Worse, (pause)

for Richer and for Poorer, (pause)

in Sickness and in Health; (pause)

Until Life's Journey Do Us Part. (pause)

Groom/Person Vows

_____ [Bride/Person Name],
Repeat After Me:

I _____ [Bride/Person Name] (pause)

Choose You _____ [Groom/Person Name] (pause)

to Be My Wedded [Husband/Wife/Spouse]; (pause)
to Share My Life in All Things. (pause)
I Will Love You and Cherish You (pause)
With Honor and Respect; (pause)
for Better and for Worse; (pause)
for Richer and for Poorer; (pause)
in Sickness and in Health; (pause)
Until Life's Journey Do Us Part. (pause)

Bride/Person Vows

The Wedding Rings

Represent Your Love and Devotion

to Each Other.

They are the Visible Sign

of an Invisible Love

That Binds Your Hearts Together.

Officiant's Intro to Rings

May I Have the Rings, Please?

(open hand and wait for rings)

Bless, O Lord, These Rings by Which

_____ [Groom/Person Name]

and

_____ [Bride/Person Name]

Have Bound Themselves to Each Other.

May the Seamless Circle of These Rings

Become the Symbol of Their Endless Love.

May it Serve to Remind Them

of the Holy Covenant

They Have Entered into Today.

Dear God, May They Live in Your Grace.

Amen

(hold open hand with rings for couple to take)

Officiant's Blessing of Rings

_____ [Groom/Person Name]

Please Place the Ring on

_____'s [Bride/Person Name] Finger,

Then Repeat After Me.

_____ [Bride/Person Name] (pause)

I Give You This Ring (pause)

as a Symbol of My Love (pause)

and a Reminder of My Promise. (pause)

With All That I Have (pause)

and All That I Am, (pause)

I Thee Wed. (pause)

Groom/Person Gives Ring

_____ [Bride/Person Name]

Please Place the Ring on

_____'s [Groom/Person Name] Finger,

Then Repeat After Me:

_____ [Groom/Person Name] (pause)

I Give You This Ring (pause)

as a Symbol of My Love (pause)

and a Reminder of My Promise. (pause)

With All That I Have (pause)

and All That I Am, (pause)

I Thee Wed. (pause)

_____
Bride/Person Gives Ring

Please Move to Each Side of Your Unity Table.

(pause until couple is in place at the table)

The Ritual of Pouring into One Vessel

Symbolizes the Joining Together and Blending

of Your Two Lives and Your Two Hearts.

Each Separate Container Represents Your Individual Lives;

Your Heritage, Your Past, Your Family, and Your Heart.

All That You Were, All That You Are, and All That You Will Ever Be.

Please Pick Up Your Sand and Pour into the Unity Vessel Together.

(pause until sand is in hands)

As You Join Your Contents Together,

You Do Not Lose Your Individualities,

But Rather, Join Your Love for Each Other

Into One Strong Union

Throughout Life's Challenges and Successes.

(pause until sand pouring is complete)

Please Join Me at the Altar.

(pause until couple is in place at the altar)

Sand Unity

Please Move to Each Side of Your Unity Table.

(pause until couple is in place at the table)

Lighting the Unity Candle

Symbolizes the Joining Together and Blending

of Your Two Lives and Your Two Hearts.

The Light of Each Outer Candle Represents Your Individual Lives;

Your Heritage, Your Past, Your Family, and Your Heart.

All That You Were, All That You Are, and All That You Will Ever Be.

Please Pick Up Your Outer Candles and Light the Unity Candle Together.

(pause until outer candles are in hands)

As You Join Your Lights Together,

You Do Not Lose Your Individualities,

But Rather, Join Your Love for Each Other

Into One Strong Union

Throughout Life's Challenges and Successes.

(pause until unity candle lighting is complete)

Please Join Me at the Altar.

(pause until couple is in place at the altar)

Unity Candle

Today isn't Just the Joining
of Two Hearts in Love,
It is the Coming Together
as a Family Unit as Well.

We Recognize and Acknowledge
the Significance of Their [Child/Children];

_____ [Name/s]

_____ [Name/s]

Recognition of Children

✝

... Let Us Pray ...

Dear Lord,

As the Wedded Couple

Walk Down This Path,

We Ask That You Light Their Way

So They May Keep

Their Eyes Focused on Your Will,

Their Hands Held Fast to Your Truth,

Their Feet Firmly Planted in Your Word,

and Their Hearts Bound Together by Your Love.

Help Them to Honor and Keep the Promises

Made Here Today, and Remind Them Daily

of Your Great Love for Them Both.

This We Pray in Your Name.

Amen

Officiant's Closing Prayer

_____ [Groom/Person Name]

and

_____ [Bride/Person Name]

May the Sun of Many Days and Years

Shine Upon You.

May the Love You Have for Each Other

Grow and Hold You Close.

May Your Dreams Come True,

and When They Don't,

May New Dreams Arise.

(continue poem on next page)

Officiant's Closing Words, part 1

Many Years from Now,

May You Look at the Other

and Be Able to Say,

"Because of You, I Have Lived the Life

I Always Wanted to Live.

Because of You, I Have Become the Person

I Longed to Be."

Officiant's Closing Words, part 2

By the Power Vested in Me;

By the [State/County] of

_____ [State/County Name];

I Now Pronounce You

_____

[Husband and Wife] / [Partners in Life] / [Married]
[Husband and Husband] / [Wife and Wife]

You May Now Kiss!

(pause for the kiss)

Please Face Your Family and Friends

(pause as the couple turns)

Ladies and Gentlemen,
It is My Honor to Present to You,
United in Marriage,

_____ [Mr./Mrs./First Name]

and

_____ [Mr./Mrs./First Name]

_____ [Last Name/s]

(wedding is complete; step aside so photographer can take photos)

Presentation

www.ingramcontent.com/pod-product-compliance
Lightning Source LLC
Chambersburg PA
CBHW051937210526
45473CB00006B/2284